Robin Liner's
YOUR OWN LITTLE
SILLY MCGILLY

Illustrated by
Madalyn V. Rogers

 CRAZY GOOD READERS ™

A Publishing Division of
East Stream Group, LLC   Weaverville, NC

Your Own Little Silly McGilly
by Robin Liner

Library of Congress Control Number: 2013954002
ISBN: 9780991034208

East Stream Group, LLC
46 Bonnie Brae Drive
Weaverville, NC 28787
www.crazygoodreaders.com

Would you like me to tell you how to become your own little Silly McGilly?

First, get red and pink
and purple and green...

...orange and blue and yellow too.

Then mix them together and soon you will be your own little Silly McGilly.

Now get shiny and slimy and gunky and junky...

...sticky and smelly with strawberry jelly, then bumpy and lumpy, and soon you will be...

...your own little
Silly McGilly.

Now start hopping and jumping and skipping and bumping...

...and twirling
and dancing and
spinning and
prancing.

Then leap and
flip and soon you
will be...

...your own little
Silly McGilly.

Now you're smiling and giggling and laughing and wiggling...

...you're singing and chuckling like you kissed a duckling...

...you're hugging and snuggling and you've just become your own little Silly McGilly.

...your own little
Goofy McSnoofy?

Think About It.

1. What did Silly have for lunch?
2. What kind of pet does Silly have?
3. Whose shoes do you think Silly is wearing at the end of the book?

Let's describe things!

When Silly McGilly played dress up…

1. What color were her shoes? Name something else that is red.
2. What color were her gloves? Name something else that is pink.
3. What color was her hat? Name something else that is green.

Play Like Silly McGilly.

1. Jump like Silly. Name something else that jumps.
2. Spin like Silly. Name something else that spins.
3. Skip and dance like Silly.

About the Author

Robin Liner is a wife, mother of six, and an entrepreneur. She has been actively engaged as a home educator for almost 20 years. She started writing children's books to help build her son's reading fluency. He was diagnosed with dyslexia at age nine and is now the most avid reader of all her kids. She lives with her family in the mountains of North Carolina.

About the Illustrator

Madalyn V. Rogers grew up in a family of artists and musicians, and she was only nine when she completed her first commissioned piece of artwork. Since then, she has painted countless murals, pieces of furniture, mailboxes, signs, sets, and faces, and earned a BFA in Drawing at the University of North Carolina at Asheville. This is the first time she has illustrated a children's book, and she loved it so much she can't wait to do the next one. She is married to David and together they have 4 children. They live in the glorious western North Carolina mountains.

Made in the USA
Charleston, SC
10 April 2014